AD LUMEN PRESS

American River College

TRACI GOURDINE

RINGING IN THE WILD

Poems

Ad Lumen Press | Sacramento | 2015

Cover image includes *Iconscape* (1997) (detail) by Keith Mayerson
and photography by Marie Mockett, used by permission.

Title page photograph by Miriam Berkley, used by permission.

For information address: Ad Lumen Press
American River College | 4700 College Oak Drive, Sacramento, CA 95841
www.adlumenpress.com
Part of the Los Rios Community College District

Library of Congress Cataloging-in-Publication Data

Gourdine, Traci L.
[Poems. Selections]
  Ringing in the wild : poems / Traci Gourdine. — First U.S. edition.
      pages ; cm
  ISBN 978-0-9911895-4-0 (trade pbk.) — ISBN 978-0-9911895-5-7 (Kindle)
  I. Title.
  PS3607.O894A6 2015
  811'.6—dc23

                              2015010393

First U.S. Edition 2015

To Mara & Tyne

RINGING IN THE WILD

TABLE OF CONTENTS

1. Smoking with Bette Davis

2. Learning the Land

1. SMOKING WITH BETTE DAVIS

In the In-Between

If you want to hear a story
you'll have to sit here
in the dark with me
outside of your own
here

In the in-between of now and then
memory and forgotten
the place between lies and truth
synapse and thought
before one mood chases the other
now to then

That moment of breath before the kiss
the feel before the tears
yes the silence before the noise

In this in-between
I stand on stage removed
from life and away
from next

The in-between of thinking it up
and writing it down
The in-between of liking what's spilled
and crossing it out

This is the place of story, of poem, of song
words tossed into air
a spectacle like stars flung to falling

I try to forget the me in this
to find meaning in the space in between each letter
each word, line, apostrophe and comma

Breathe the in-between
the rise of eyes
the dip to page
the inhale and exhale

What I have found
in the in-between begins
like this

Small Warmth

She thinks he gestures to some other
exhales and sinks back deep
like a turtle peaceful in her waters

For what rises from the soul?
To see the tundra of fluorescence
aisles, cereal boxes, rude staring children
with eyes nude as eggs?

She waits her turn at the cashier's line
Knows what will be
her dinner
where it will be eaten
what small warmth it will bring
how the tail end of day will wag
its way through a crevice of hill
drain her walls
and night will fall for sure
steady as her own sleeping breath

Stuck there in the middle of the way
he clears his throat
An old song plays the back of his ear
He feels some dance left
in the hollow of his bones
some light, some flicker seizes him

He is glad again amongst this monotony
tiled floors and rubber soles
coupons and half crate eggs
Mondays following Sundays
like dumplings follow chicken
like hell follows heaven

In this moment
he becomes visible to himself again
and he looks out as if roused
from some long sick

Perhaps it is her hair
The way strands tremble there
above her heartbeat
Perhaps it is her lonely stance
How she holds herself still with such gentle hands
glum yet patient and standing it all

He sees how each finger rests
light upon her flesh
bringing him to imagine
to hope

somehow she might lean
might offer up
just a small part of her peace
in just the same measure

Lola's Red Dress

This is the noise of softening day
Scattered newspapers drift limp over bellies
The radio scratches a Holiday tune
as Lola takes the stairs two at a time
The banister strobes the black of her bare feet
Small dust storms rise with every gesture
All a swirl of sudden and frantic

Upstairs sister lowers a red dress
over breasts, hips
crimson above her knees

She is a rush of hair and cloth
She is busy with her imagining
dim lights and him
How she'll drift towards his ground to settle

Sister disappears into woman
dark brown and ripe
She folds wildness into grace

I forget
Lola slamming doors and cutting her eyes
I've seen her hands fierce and impatient
pulling weeds, my hair, gutting chickens and fish

At dawn Lola slips from red to brown
Her memories trail the floor
shoes, slip, nylons snagged and useless
fall to the dark
between window and doorway
all ordinary and sure

Lola
brown with white bra and panties
Lola
brown with dark hair and eyes
with mother and father
with sister who stares from lids half closed

She will sleep and rise
as before
waiting out her days
for nights
a drift of cloth stained red

A Woman Knows

I

A woman knows
it's on when
a fist unfurls

She stands on tentative legs to test this
    new air about her
careful that this is not some trick to fool
her onto ground that slides
out from under
her

    Again

She inventories
tired bras, proletariat panties
trades them in for lingerie
    sleek cool satins
    delicate lace made of thin air
all worth a month's salary
all for him

Looks good in her mind
She imagines it all tossed
torn, pulled aside in haste
Her strappy little needle thin heels
        she can't catch a bus in
        walk down stairs in
        just sit pretty   pearl-tipped pink toes in
are worn to bed

because the entire effect
        all that suggestion   all that promise
just won't let him wait

Seems plausible
Seems sensible
Somehow
it's on again

II

A woman knows to count her blessings
when she sees the failed
couples hard faced and bored
eyes averted over tablecloths
while his fingers brush hers

Her mother has been silenced
is more satisfied than even she
and listen
sisters no longer worry
coast to coast   cajoling and coaxing
as if she were a mule stubborn on a hill

A woman knows to keep the peace
as holidays arrive in quick succession
        There is no choice but to settle in
        try it on   let it ride   test it out
        be someone's someone
a Taken-Care-of Woman
no one has to worry about

She's a WE
not an   I
        but a THEY

a PAIR

not a single
        but a two setting
now a Two-for-One

no more solo flights

                and

        single is as good as

            ANON

III

A woman knows
it's over when

the sound of his breathing makes her want
                to smother him
                        not gently
but firmly and for sure

the way a shoe snuffs a bug

The weight of his hands on her flesh makes her tremble
                the way mares shiver beneath flies
        so she ducks, runs circles, raises dust
bristles at the smacking sounds
kisses in her ear

There's a shame in this
        a quiet   guilty   bad girl   woman mother
turning back to whore
kinda shame in this

What she had once prayed for and received she now
        rejects
        keeping her   quiet

in the dark

She lies
arms to sides   ankles crossed
beneath the covers
so she won't   kick
won't twitch   won't move   or buck

so she can concentrate on the soft
calm of her own breath

hear the steady
            rise and fall
rising and falling
        days, like leaves
                like dreams, like promises
                all tides above

the clang

in her heart

Moving Out of Rhythm

On steamy nights when all goes still
women become long shadows
watching familiar men
light and gather noisily

crows on wires
men on front stoops

In the hour before dusk
when night is thrown back by neon
her reflection ripples the glass
She is measuring the laughter
the bar room, pool hall, card game
had me a fancy girl last night
lost my job, don't give a damn
kind of laughter
for its danger
its warning of what may come

It rises like steam off of pavement
disappearing into choked memory
Men lapse into weary thoughts
nodding their heads
switching then to soft chuckles
whispered curses

as hands clench steadily within
empty pockets

Resigned eyes watch cars
watch the turn of newspapers
rolling loose and free in the street

Things seem uglier now
harder than twenty minutes ago

At this late hour
eyes shoot a glance
upward
at curtains
aware of a sudden flutter
out of rhythm
with the beat
of the night

Smoking with Bette Davis

When I was fifteen, I tried to smoke with Bette Davis
I wasn't a practiced smoker. I usually puffed
without inhaling
But after many scenes, I took to swallowing smoke
in gulps without the choke and burn
Blew clumsy smoke rings at the ceiling
Layered ropes of plume above my lip
waving my wrist, leaning back in the chair
slumped elegant like her
tossed mink

I couldn't keep up
The gray of old movie strobed across my face
I was fifteen then and wondering
if Bette could be true
Raised from infancy to brittle eyed woman
and not giving a damn what the neighbors thought
Oh, I could be her, I decided
at least until my parents returned
throwing on the lights, clattering their shoes across the
        floor

I could be her, I thought
baring my teeth at men like a feral cat
wanting nothing but a light and then to be left alone

I could be her with a practiced walk and turn of the
       wrist

Bette Davis
Bette Davis
Bette Davis

Filling the room with her smoke
Blowing each word in heat and exhale
Never dropping an ash or torching a mattress

Bette would lose like a poor sport
sprinting down highways
her shadow in the weeds
shoulders heaving
hair crisscrossed about her face
And always in sorrow, always
Bette's eyes would still hate the world
stubborn to stone and wanting a cigarette
I could be her

I've felt like her after mild disasters
and endless tiresome parties
during and after men with soggy matches and broken
       lighters

when buses broke down in rainstorms
and the last plane has left to Paris
while waiting under dim street lights
or in bath water gone gray and cold

I have been Bette in the weeds before
Sucking up the last of my tears
while looking for my lost cigarette
I have been Bette, slamming bedroom doors
while rooting through the dark
for my lost cigarette

It always seems to come out better somehow
tears and nicotine slide easier than regret or apologies
a slow black burn
in the back of my throat

Baby Got On

One of her legs is resting across a chair
girl teenager with the weeds setting in
she could lick your fingers
and tell you favorite stories
her straw words blowing
air ill-shaped with light

In Chicago the night bears wages
and she hunkers down
to fold as compact as nylons
careful to avoid getting torn

She wears other people's hair
walks down stairs trailing dark grins
sheet of ice
pillow of razors
her blue-black eyeliner is streaming

She's learned this much
some rules are simpler than others:

chew words of violence then swallow hard
laugh when you fall off the curb
it can be a long train ride home don't sleep

man is the name giver
listen

Daughter Revealed

Upon this weight the dusk
The small outline of girl on bed edge
Girl-silk, splay-legged, listening to the radio
She is a rag doll

tired bones soft in solitude
like the city itself in ripe spring
By the time you read this
she will be gone to another year

You know that
her waiting is abandoned
Don't even watch or listen
leaving girls trail nothing

only pleasure and awkward strutting
hair undone like scarves
child gestures contained and mute
Her father has the brightest vision

something he can recall for years
moist curls, cereal stains, torn knees
all now a spark of memory
Little girl gone to woman

off to the steep carnal overflow
the boys from Queens flick
their lighters and have a look
There is beauty in her eyes

a thousand kisses no one wants
She is out there looking
sweat, dew, saliva, blood
bare cheeked, she smolders

When They Stop Watching You

You get that knowing look in your eye
Shaded lids lowered in boredom
the body slouches, reclines
tired of the endless waiting to be free
suddenly awake with
smarts no one else has
visions only you can see

Now you wait, watching me
believing me predictable
and just going through my seasons
Just some sturdy predictable oak
making buds, sprouting leaves
making colors, going naked
and showing the aches and scars
of my winters

You've seen my entire routine
You think I'm done
Now you're waiting
with a sullen impatient stillness
radio on and the TV too loud
seeing how'd you do it better
avoiding the marks I've made
from NYC to California

prints for you to follow
not wasting time, avoiding
the shit of myths, hormones, the fables of men

Little daughter, you should know
I'm not through making my prints
my eyes hood daily with plans
Toes and fingers twitch at the ready
and watch this, I can play the radio
louder than you when nobody's home
love songs, traveling songs, rollicking
gonna get past the blahs songs
and I sing and sing
swaying like always
It never fades

Near Grant's Tomb

boys whistle when you walk by
they bring their fingers to their mouths in salute
there are so many of them
wild with colors bought on the avenue
red pants green shoes orange suits
strange birds long legged and swift
they know how to swoop without wings

you turn, you turn
alone in a window
flickering your shadow
like thoughts light as bones
they can't reach you from here
only the sounds of cooing and screeching
only the crash of desperation on pane

sweet faced boys pose on the stoop
sometimes they let you pass
at daylight
the silk of skin on the ankle ripples
pleasure
this is the caress of slow blinking eyes

pregnant ones walk free
closed to discovery but open to wreckage
they are listening to the pulse of waters

so beautiful with their moon-faced stares
the sidewalks go silent as they pass

moist mouse
tender in the belly
you might as well get used to it
this is the hunting ground
they are waiting to greet you

from spaces of dark, a hot breeze unfurls
in whispered loneliness
your names follow you
blood slick and full of sorrow

Four Cornered

I

My mother is uneasy. The vacuum cleaner gets on her nerves. Sucking. Sucking the invisible dirt gathered in silence. Shadows of blue twitch her eyelids. TV voices whisper scream despite her sleep. In April trees creak the back fence in a whine until July calls the cicada to sing stranger songs. My footfalls startle her away from windows. The curtains swing this truth. Mail remains unopened. Her name warps with rain.

II

My sister is uneasy. Her son won't sleep in the dark. He crowds her bed as if they are poor again. He has made her aware of shadows. Her new kitchen is painted an odd blue, causing reflections to smear. No paint can cover that shade. On New Year's Eve she paid $50.00 in advance for recorded music, flat champagne and another year of loneliness. Snow blinds her exit; it blocks her return. She is so successful she can plan her own death. With a Do-It-Yourself book she can force her will in four easy steps. Physicians must pull the plug. Her body is cremated and strewn across water. All belongings will go to Mother. I will be given her son to rock in the dark.

III

My father is uneasy. His blindness has erased all sense of time. He calls across the country at odd hours only to apologize. He wakes his ex-wife, his daughters, their husbands. Babies wail in the background. Dogs dig up his front lawn, but he doesn't know whom to blame. Computers, tape recorders, devices for the blind breakdown. He is thrown back into himself unable to work for hours. His new wife wants to redecorate after finding the vasectomy irreversible. His dark glasses never hide his confusion. He tilts his head to measure the meaning of sounds: shuffled paper, coughs, sighs, and hesitant footsteps. He knows these dense pauses reveal truth better than image. He hopes none of us realize how advantageous this is.

IV

I am uneasy. My mother's voice is coming out of my mouth. She leads my hands as I braid my daughter's hair. When I drive the car with crying children, her fingers grip the wheel and the world recedes. Her habit of replies are now mine, faint smiles, a courteous goodbye, and everyone is satisfied. In winter I sense my sister walk within my bones. Her lowered eyed endurance stays through spring. She has taught me how to smile and grind back teeth. I have been practicing the walk of the blind. The world is made of so much air; cluttered with sharp corners that bark, layered with sounds I hear best with eyes closed. I am aware that the world has sudden drops. And spirits of the living hover near.

2. LEARNING
THE LAND

Learning the Land

I was insolent and bored
when faced with earth
Raised on concrete half my life
with hardly a slit of sky visible
above my head, I swore only pigeons
ragged blue jays claimed the sky

But in northern California
I had to be taught to see all over again
The language of this land is
the swollen river
ribbon of tule fog
white caps in April sea
muddied old horse patient
in rain

I've come to know
how to find the dark seams
on an orchard's horizon
and watch serrated black wings of crow
fly their eastern commute
in from their daily work
somewhere west of me

They light, stand tall, yellow
black eyes set

in the direction they will fly
and they mingle there on the ground
like blue-collar steel workers in taverns
until they all rush up to climb the bruising sky
Not even the best of us can rise
so fast so determined without the need
of a backward glance at ground

Central Avenue

Barbershops and hair salons
lounges and old movie houses
drugstores, rib joints, pizza, sub shops
cheap tacky clothes stores where you could buy
shimmy, shimmy, sheer see-through black blouses
over a fire engine red bra

On every corner the brothas pause to slap hands
eyes always on the street
tippin' on   tippin' on
past little girls in braids clipped down in
yellow, green, blue barrettes
racing around adult legs
dragging baby brothers and jump ropes
exotic names pierce the air
Latwanne, Miyeeka, Janisha
sometimes simply Brenda
arguments punctuated with "IMMA TELL!"
quieted as they round corners

Dogs on three legs miraculously dodge
huge, huge, long boat cars gleaming
iridescent green and gold
station wagons full up with grandma in curlers
Pops chewing a stub of a cigar

with a ladder hanging out the back
honking at two women ignorant to the light change
eyes closed and singing to the radio

Above the street sit the meaty
arms of women lean into sunlight
Sentries of the avenue in faded Woolworth dresses
obese with the gossip, they watch the whores
take up the space where shadows may fall

Neon flickers on dusk
dirty pinks, faint greens, champagne bubbles come to
        life
Lucky 12, Terrace Lounge, Kitty Corner, The Fabre
all lit up with jukeboxes, pool tables
large bodies on stools hunch over
waiting   waiting   they turn bored eyes to stare
at silhouettes of moving landscape

Young men practice the walk
black hats crumpled upon closely shaved heads
jeans scrape the ground below black high tops
combs stuck in pocket ready
for that pause, that pose of quick picking
a duck to peer in reflection and take a stab at vanity

They'll couple up with sudden dates
outside movie houses
karate films, stale popcorn
young girls popping gum, snapping Juicy Fruit in time
with the crisp click of thin heeled shoes
hair gleaming, lips glossed, nails longer
than they were this afternoon
so red, so orange, so purple
sure to catch some attention
in the dark

They scatter past drunks lost in mumbled curses
traffic lights blinking solemn yellow
making it impossible to judge a chance swagger
sway across the street

The night is left to cruising cops, hurting habits
fools without sense to know the party's over
and the whores watch from shadows
step out in unison
in silence arms crossed about their hollow waists
wounded daughters of the avenue

Calculated Glimpses
on the East Side Train

I know how to swim the deadly zone
pass men on hot days
making music with their lips
twisting suggestion with their hands
in a homage to their loneliness

It's too easy on the sidewalk
I like the ground shaking buck
the rush of steel on steel
I like the soft rocking drift
towards brink's edge
the theory of anonymity
and I like you

You are looking at me
at me and away
away and at me

Rhythm of glimpses
rhythm of slow smiles
lean   cross your denim legs and empty your arms
roll   swing in certain stride and throw your shadow
        over me

I watch
speed and light twist your features
coming events
comfort and torture   comfort and torture
tossed down at my side

In this temporary respite
no promises
no signs of relief or danger

just this
blind chance with closed eyes

Father Faith

I

On Sundays he would wake the house
With God. A voice louder than any rock station
Found all of us
Beneath our covers.
How gracious is it really
How should the children come
To love God if his name
Blisters their sleep?

II

After the comics are read
Three sisters have their hair braided tight
Tight along the tender of their scalp
Dressed in rough heavy tights, cramped
Patent leather with bows
All three of us prepped for sitting
In a row
Legs swinging in a pew

Not a single one of us understood why
We dressed for someone
Everyone feared

III

Daddy tried a different place
This time my mother wouldn't come
In this place the words were lilting
Like songs wanting to be sung
Hebrew. Temple. And now
Church on Saturdays
With Daddy upstairs in the place
Of dark coats and slope-shouldered quiet men
Wearing sad faces so different than
The tight-lipped mean from before

I recall their long white scarves
And the scrolls carefully unfurled
Gently passed from hand to hand
Men humming a language we could hear
Through the pipes where we took our
Hebrew lessons and learned
Dreidel songs

IV

When enough funerals played out
 Caskets led by mules, limousines jammed with flowers
A New Orleans trumpeter far behind playing blues
When enough women wore black on TV
Mourning with Coretta so still in her blackness

When a child saluted the passing of the dead
And his mother reeled him in
Mother in black, Jackie in black
Her small daughter staring at a shadow
Tracing the ground
When Malcolm was shot dead in a church
Amongst the faithful and devoted
Under the knowing gaze of a god
All of us kids wanted the cartoons to come back

Daddy stopped
Trying to find where this god lived
Stopped trying to hunt Him down
Like he was a relative we needed
To meet
Stopped hunting for him in buildings
In languages

In songs and within days of the week
He let up after that

He just stayed home
Planted himself before the TV and watched
The mouth of Cronkite
Sure and daily as any other prayer

My Mother's Worth

was in a tiny bottle elegant haze of deep, deep, blue brought back from her travels to France. Young as she was, married as she was to a hard-headed, too-self assured man, mother as she was to 4 back-to- back kids, she found herself in Paris all on her own by accident and she smiled, did not apologize as she left her husband behind in the airport because he thought she had his ticket, his passport; that she would carry him the way she carried her children's coats, wiped their butts, remembered their shoe left here and the other there, kept the dog off the couch, draped and ironed sheets, cut the crusts off bread and hid vitamins in everyone's oatmeal cuz it was her job to be the doer holder getter rememberer even if she was a woman on her way to Paris. She left my father there sputtering in the airport.

She smiled and waved her white-gloved hand over her shoulder, said, "See you later, dear. Catch up with me when you can." In Paris along the narrow beauty of the old within the tiny cafes and shops for two whole days she carried her own coat and ate no oatmeal. I still have that tiny blue bottle of French perfume she found on that trip, the perfume that held a scent of what a woman can find on her own by accident in Paris.

We Went Home After This

Our clothes flew from the roof of the car
old station wagon smelling of wood and leather
full up with us four kids
loose and rolling unhindered
like apples out of a bag

For years I wondered:
Did dark clothes fly off that car?
Did suitcases spring their jaws
cough our lives into the night?

I remember kneeling
in that backseat to view
my beautiful mother
plucking up our tossed
belongings strewn like litter

there in the street
Her face changed
at each strobe of passing headlight
I didn't know it then
but I was watching a woman
in the midst of a sudden
decision

I would only know later
at 32, then again at 35, most definitely by 40
what my mother's face in headlights meant
what the face of a woman looks like
when leaving, when running

She stood there in sweeps of car light
clothes in her arms like dirty laundry
and for a moment she looked back at us
our four faces watching
her failed escape

But This Is History

I watch TV with a bowl of popcorn
     glaciers fall into impossible blue
     but I chew on
The sun tantrums before night and
by 11pm the Gulf
has hemorrhaged again
a cascade so dense
     there is no pulse
from Louisiana to Florida
In the last Amazonian wood
the tribesmen peer up
from the nearly conquered dark
still knowing their names and refusing to give up
all that they have known
     all that we have forgotten

Fathers

All fathers were once small children
        hiding behind doors a finger to their lips

This one here lived in short pants
        feared the dogs that barked at night

His longings? Only for a small sailboat
        seen radiant in a window at the 5 and 10

Every father was once a child
        who wandered far as daylight would allow

They scavenged wheels for boards, cat's eyed marbles
        tin soldiers, kites, baseball cards

These children soon to men had dirt on their necks
        behind their ears, grass and mud spelled the day

These men, these fathers once climbed trees to build
        palaces from scraps found useless on the ground

All fathers were boys
        tinkerer without tools, reducing toasters and TVs
        to plates and screws

Watch how they whoop, row the air, arms in tilt
    down dirt roads exuberant and lifting to flight

Little boys harvested to fathers
    Imagine them, they were singing

Cantos for the
Children Lost in Travel

Dia de los Muertos, 2014

Here they come the angelitos
faces wearing echoes of their parents

We bring you flores, dulces, y pan de muertos
all for you to fill your bellies on this long night

Angelitos, come closer
we want to sing for you and rattle
the seeds of gourds to make you smile

Spill your drink, we don't mind
wipe your red mouths on your tattered sleeves
scatter the crumbs of our ofrendas across the floor
We invite you

This night is yours
in the way days should have been
with gifts at your feet and our arms around you
it is your time
come home

In This Present

My life is sleek
more graceful than the last
The leavings are easier, so gradual
I hardly feel a thing
No slamming of doors
No long last looks
Scenes simply slide into view
Constant as the bottom of sky

Sleep, wake, sleep
Inhale, exhale
Unconscious swallows
This is what it takes
to keep on walking

Is the view behind my back blank
or has a crowd gathered behind me
The dead, the old husband, relatives
All those lovers I've angered away
Behind closed doors
I turn to find simple
still life

This morning is over
It has risen into afternoon approaching twilight

so odd how the clock never leaves
a trail of seconds
Every gesture
unphotographed

A Reasonable Man

He looked young
had in his pockets
keys for doors
he could no longer open

There on the sidewalk with heat
lapping the back of his neck
he sees a vague image
himself in wilted suit
the bones of his wrists
like broken ancient
branches exposed brittle
vulnerable in his poor

He has the last taste
hope in the far
corner of his mouth
his tongue waits
to speak

He is a reasonable man
in heavy shoes
2 sizes too big
he cannot recognize
the sound of his own
footfalls to this place

Unforgiving world
let loose this poverty
this loverless state
this world of so many holding
useless keys in pockets
let loose just a little
set a cool breeze
down
allow a man entry
let him whistle
his way home
lucky this time for sure

Last Call

blood on black hands
the bars will open anyway
     compact rooms of dim
gray gloom hovers the shoulders

the bartender leans one hand on the bar
his stance forever shifting
     3 steps up
     5 strides left
     1 step back

he knows the universe
a circle of ice, gin
a circle of timeless faces
room always for one more

rain falls pity in the streets
the feel of ice on tongues appease
     holds time
     loose dreams

some get caught broken
they are dragged out
to home
without deliverance

the rest, they will rise
a stumbling
a woeful zigzag
back to you

3. BACK TO THE DEUEL

Tell Me

Tell me about when you were five and knew you had to
        grow up.
Tell me.
Tell me about one of your scars. No, that scar. The one
        that rages
across your throat. The one that ripples when you blink.
        Yeah
that's a good scar.
Tell me.
Tell me.
Tell me a secret you've never told anyone. Disguise your
        handwriting.
No one in this room will know. Crumble the paper.
Crumble it in a ball. Put it in your sock.
Recipes for burying the disappeared.
Recipes for burning buildings.
Recipes for finding the snitch.
Tell me a recurring dream.

Now write a Christmas poem for the Warden.

Bad Luck

Yesterday the smell of that place almost made me one of them…I know that particles of air from…1932…1954…'67…'78…'86…all of the air inhaled and exhaled in 2001…is trapped in that prison… Nothing gets out…Every meal…each fart…guffaw… belch…every drying mop and empty boot…thickens the air…The smell sits on your shoulders…crawls up your sleeves…combs each strand on your head…It slows your walk into a wary prowl…The eyes in your head trickle…strange tears…They burn…itch…redden…and the guards become suspicious…You are too close to the other's…side.

Not a Matinee

Sometimes I sit in the dark with them…When I have nothing to say…I turn off the lights…put my back to them…The movie has something to do with writing…I tell them…something to do with technique…Then the shooting and killing begins…a woman begins to march…across the screen…swinging her breasts… rolling her eyes…Language breaks down…screaming curses…muttered threats…insane monologues…The music throbs with warning…Something odd happens… when I play these movies inside the prison…These films alter themselves and send out the wrong images…I've never seen this part before…I don't recall that character… doing that…in my living room…The men pound the tables…rise to their feet and howl…press their faces close against the glass…Someone shouts, "Siddown man!"…They yell at the characters…slam their fists into their palms…during the good parts…scowl…at botched homicides…bungled robberies…laugh with heads thrown back…when a car slams into a wall, careens off a cliff…The movie is writing over itself…A faint whir from…switches and buttons turned on…high…When it's over they smile…at me…in the most grateful way… exhausted…spent and sated…They never ever ask me… what the point was

In This Place

There are snitches whispering
Weight lifters ready to die over rusted iron
Street vs. yard smarts
Protective custodies uneasy with the silence

A world of religion swirls in denim blue
Christians, Muslims, Buddhists, Jews, Jehovah
        Witnesses
vying to crowd out each other's god

In this place the body and mind is force fed
food and education
pancakes mixed with latex gloves
jelly spread with industrial paintbrushes
drums of powdered milk, eggs, juice, mayonnaise
water swirling with rainbow colors
Brutal men in hairnets slam potatoes on the tray

The math teacher drinks from a flask
Elderly English teachers cat fight in the faculty lounge
Inmates brush their stubbled scalps watching
        unconcerned
No heroes in this place
No one will jump in

Everyone is waiting for the true war to begin

A man's shadow can move 200 times around the yard
2 different stories, guilt and innocence are told 5,000
        different ways
4,000 televisions strobe 32,000 walls
2 minute phone calls are replayed like mantras
There are 700 ways to say,
        goodbye
        hello
        fuck you
        marry me
        can I come home

Chant

In moments of desperation he writes
mojo on scraps of paper bag
out of view from the prison guards

Their keys and hard heeled boots set off alarms
warnings hiss from to cell to cell
"Man walkin'…Man walkin'…"

Inmates feign nonchalance
poses of reading
poses of prayer
poses of sleep

Vincent has three pennies on a paper bag
pours a trickle of honey across worn faces
a chant he's carried in him
from the green hills of North Carolina

He tries to call on mojo
after all of these miles
He knows a crucial step is missing
He knows it's in a gesture
an ingredient missing and forgotten

One white candle / three pennies / piece of brown
        paper
little honey / nine consecutive days / visualize
        freedom
thank the Creator /

Fisherwoman

Fisherwoman in a cell
casts out line after line to the dim
rooms, sad empty homes with men
awake and staring forward
the ones awake and forgetting why
Joanna sends a lure out to the ones
who press brows against steering wheels
drunk at intersections blinking yellow lights
men who can't dance   can't remember how

Joanna needs a place to light
Eight years done with six months to go
she sets the net for the one
who will let her stay just long enough to get
her bearings and a new dress, and some earrings
a haircut better than Betty's dull scissors can give
She needs someone to take her out, fill her up
tell her more than her own mirror or hands can
about what a woman is, can do, can bring
can break in a man

In the dayroom, Joanna lays out her catch
laughing at the photos sent
ignoring the faces of men
their trembling overexposed smiles

She eyes the background
sizing up the goods
cars and TVs, a rose bush neat
along aluminum siding
She picks one photo, sets the others free
Floats them out into stagnant air
for the others in need of a nibbler

They Come

They come   in slippers and denim
                 singing loud to earphones
                 or simply air
                 or saying nothing at all

They come   trailing their gaze along the ground
                 sweeping the walks with the stroll
                 sizing up a possible slip out
                 a possible gamble
                 but giving up again because it's no use

They come   with nothing
                 no pens, pencils, no paper
                 just a plastic comb from the commissary
                 and maybe a worn out letter
                 scrawled in a child's hand
                 creased and creased to fit
                 in a pocket

They come   in tired
                 rings of gray beneath their eyes
                 limbs heavy and swinging boneless
                 because inside anything solid
                 will be broken

They come   with an anger smell
             in the sweat
             the gloss of rage smears
             their lips

They come   in shy and ready for shame
             chins casting shadows
             down the front of themselves
             like a spirit stain

They come   with the last phone call in their eyes
             clenching their fists knotting their jaws
             after the latest turn down from the Board
             unfinished sentences in their mouths
             sitting with their backs to the wall

They come   on time
             in late
             in hollow
             dragging memories in by the heels
             and up by the roots

They come   from all day low down dollar jobs
             at the laundry
             in the kitchen
             skin cracked like August earth
             skin smelling
             of boiled chicken and Ajax
             from the scrubbing of dayrooms
             from the scrubbing of bathrooms
             from digging tired whored earth

These sisters of trouble
             come and gather
             together they come to
             they come to
             they try

Not All of Him is Gone

This Chicano carries the words of his barrio etched deep… within his skin…on his knuckles he wraps La Raza…in black ink…LA sits on his thumb…RAZA follows on each digit…he flexes this fist often…sometimes I see him stroke the words…softly…sometimes he rubs at it hard…when frustration or loneliness hits…pushing the ink deep…inside his blood…Jokey practices his stroll…when he comes to class…for five seconds…he is on…a Fresno Saturday night boulevard…and I am Lucha…Anna…Maria…Gloria…Sylvia…the one with high black hair…earrings of gold that glint…at the flash and pass…of low riding gold rimmed stereo throbbing cars…heavy with song and impatience…I am the one… fresh from church…a novena falling from my lips…with lowered eyes and red brown skin…with crooked teeth and one homemade dress…he will follow me home… teach me a new prayer…I am the one…who walks in between mother and father…protected like a horse in a stall…He whispers my name…a slow stroke across my cheek…he finds me in windows…three stories up… leaning deep into the night…to watch him pass…in this place…I am all of these girls…to him…their faces blur…within mine…their giggles echo…in my eyes… my gestures…I carry memories of these girls to him… in a place of sharp curses…hard touches…and lengthy silence…the stench of bland food…old tears…broken promises…fade memory into myth…when Jokey crosses the dayroom for class…his face softens…he sets his eyes in such a way…I must remember to smile.

Short Dog

The heat wave the solitude
The broken cracks between weeping
And laughing broke him
When nothing else could

Voices on the tier hum like a heart song
In the womb he found the rhythm there
Curled tight around himself he learned
The new language raining down
From cells three stories up and two below

He imagined himself in a tenement   a high rise barrio
A quick hotel room in West Hollywood   maybe
        Chicago
Right beside a Greyhound station shuts his eyes
He slept knees to chest imagining tomorrow
This long sleep might end

Eyes in the corridor watch
Guards have sounds only they can carry:
Keys swinging free and loose
Hard heels measuring the tiers
Nonchalant whistling
Deadly friendly like a bored cop in a
Midwest town

All of this broke him

He was broken   this Short Dog
His mother knew him as Mijo
The one who would not sit still
8 year old pachuco with a fist that never opened
Except to steal
She tried to break him but he threw her
Like he threw bullies, teachers, cops
A neighbor went to the hospital
Short Dog went to jail

He went to jail
He went home
He went back to jail
He made his way home
He went to jail
He went back
Home
To prison to stay

His urge for the outs stopped
Women, hot dogs
The feel of jumping steel
Beds, cars, guns

He didn't miss the nights
Surviving the strobe of avenue
What a slow passing car might mean

This place broke him of the outs
Stripped him down off his cool
Gave him slate walls painted 63 coats of gray
Gave him echoes
Choked back tears and laughter straining
To get out

He has a dim naked bulb over his head
To light a new world around him
And once when turning a corner
A pile of hard wool blankets one flat pillow
A towel a roll of toilet paper heaped
Into his arms Short Dog saw
The longest corridor in the world

No women
No red cars, no corona, jalapenas in oil
Aho!

If life means regret
If 25 to forever means more broken teeth

With only his knuckles to shield the sharp
Short Dog decided to make a new luck
Take on another walk
Own this corridor, make it home
Get born somehow from cinder
This the new mother home

Without Waving Goodbye

1 Mother

My car throbs from the run
Twitching from the race
Between diesels and Geos

I drive cussing at near misses
Say tiny prayers for the dead
at the side of the road

Radio music sweeps the wind
pass Stockton, tire farms, muddy cows
blinking at the flat heat

Earth heaves a prison
between concrete and railroad tracks
I respond with relief at its sight
because I didn't die back there
but now my soul holds her breath
knowing voluntary lockdown comes next
For awhile I'll lose everything
then reclaim it at the gate
If it's okay with Them

I park and sit staring
My pregnant belly thumps restless

beneath the guard's tower
aimed and watching any false move
from my last cigarette

II Mother & Child

Here's our little girl all dressed up
Like a birthday cake frothy pink
ringed in lace
topped off with two red bows

Patent leathers chase down dull pennies
hidden from the unlucky
All grown up and in bad trouble
I tug at her hand smooth her hair
pull too hard on her arm
to sit
to sit down   be still
Why don't cha wait here
Be quiet now

And the pretty little dress
sits and sits stiffly bored

while the guard empties my purse
claws through gum wrappers
bobby pins
a lone penny rolls across the floor

And it feels scary here
the way shadows fall
behind faces humbled
smothered coughs
a choked giggle a vague apology
as we snatch back loose dignity
when the visiting hour begins

III Child In Tow

Barefoot
A smear of face
after a long day in the car
Jogging after momma
always talks to me
without turning around
lips moving on the other side of her head
as she walks fast away from that place
It looks like a mean giant's castle

cavernous, strange
In its grip, a gray man with a faint smile
someone from a snapshot
torn, gone yellow
a person with hesitant eyes
My father
A vague threat behind a tiny window

IV Color It Away

I've got a cookie pressed close to my chest
It smells funny
Slid across the table after I draw
A gift
For them I make scratchy kitty faces
Then sometimes big men
Blank faces
Long mouths of swirling holes
Claws for hands
It's nice they say
Broken cookies
Broken crayons
Crumbled words between grownups
The silence is my chewing
and trying to swallow

V Child No More

Not enough money for skates
Money for gas
The old cars
jumbled with kids and achy old women

Every Saturday it's the same road
For years the air foul with exhaust
This ride never ends

She says, "Mija, grab your shoes
You can put them on in the car
Take your books, your favorite doll
Hurry, mija, we are late
He's always waiting in that crowd
for you"

She forgets that I am 17
That we now bleed in sync
That my breasts ache at the slightest touch
My eyes are curious
no longer wide with acceptance

She says, "Remember to kiss him
when you go in don't hang back that way;
you hurt his feelings Smile a little, tell him
about school Don't mumble
you have such a pretty voice
Mija, do you hear?"

Serena's party is at the roller rink
Boys and girls practice cool
slouching macho on skates
Music blares with unheard of love
for the girls who know makeup, kissing
how to walk without a stumble
My hands have never held such invitations
I walk school halls without a name
Eyes straight ahead
I move through lines unknown

She says, "You should write him more
He misses your letters
The old ones are yellow on the wall
Take him those pictures of you and Elena
The one with you so pretty by the lake

Let him see you grow, mija, it's not right
he should miss so much"

Everything is about to ripen
Snapshots are shields against the missing
Distant shadows speed across the lens
I am not the child who takes pride in missing teeth
I am not the one who wears hearts in her hair
A daughter is slowly dying, and Momma
the absent no longer interests me

Back to the Deuel

I started teaching in the sane world
community college of even rowed desks
students free to come and go

We were talking about the death penalty
One blonde girl, freckled and grinning, said
"Kill them, kill them all"
She fanned her thighs in her seat
winged them as she leaned forward
"Kill them good, those monsters"

That night I drove the highway one last time
back to the prison, not as instructor
but as special guest. My role had changed
into distinguished visitor. I was free
to roam, to touch, to speak openly
with men kept at bay for 10 years

That night in full view, I touched a monster
for the first time. Marveled at the soft
of his cheeks where two perfect dimples rode
And then, excited as Helen Keller, I sidestepped
released that one and went to another
felt the dome of his brown head
commenting on how skin held tight as cellophane

the play of dancing dots
of institutional lights upon his black head

This monster let me touch
feel what was left of his braids
stood patient and still in case I frightened away
held himself still while the others grinned

Then another came near
The one with a butterfly stitch on his right eye
"What happened to you Scrappy? You fightin' again?"
I held him there, his eyes wary
grin stiff across his teeth
I tamed his arm, gripped it
the way his mother had frowned in his eyes
while I touched each wound he earned

Old scars as stories
falls from windows, bar stools
the failed exploits on the streets
years inside this cave

Torn ear, split lip, sad hard wounds on his knuckles
I traced the ones I wondered about
right there, unrestrained and glad

I was the one returned
as if from some long solitude

I ran my hands rough, up and down their arms
pounded playfully on their chests, hard
enough to rock a few back on their state issued heels
Oh how they laughed surprised at my gall
I fisted my hands and swung at the sides of their
        massive arms

I was free now. Free to stroll and touch
those I had come to know so well
with words, through words
They confessed; I cajoled
We made pretty lies and screamed
at one another in laughter

Brothers and one sister
Students and teacher
Writers and writer
Monsters and Little Red Riding Hood
skipping her basket of words up and down
the highway

Ten years of unbroken time

All so worth it
this final goodbye

Barred Tongue

I'm a political prisoner of the United States of America.

This place makes me ashamed, see. I'm nothin' like these
guys.

And then they came at me, busted through my door, so
I hit the guy. He got 15 stitches; I got 17 years.

It never fails. Whenever I start a meaningful
relationship, I get locked up.

Most of the brotha's in here are musicians.

I'm up for parole in May. My folks say there's a job for
me at Disney World. Would you recognize me as
Mickey Mouse?

I don't know, I think my heart is breaking. This
loneliness carries a big knife and wears steel-toed
boots.

What's the difference inside or out? The whole world's
gonna end any damn way.

You smell like my mother. Guard Williams smells like

my first date, and the warden reminds me of my fifth
    grade teacher.

Every Friday is fish day, Sunday means pork and beans,
    Thursday is mac and cheese. Who needs a calendar
    with a steady diet like this?

I'm from Queens. I ain't never been to California. But
    somehow they say, I got an arm that stretches
    three thousand miles.

You like the ponies? I got a friend out here with a horse.
    You bet him third race for fifty; ya can't lose.

I'm never gettin' outta here. Not ever.

You look nice today.

Did you cut your hair?

Girl, you putting' on some weight?

Say, can you give me a cigarette? Nah, a real cigarette;
    the kind with a name on 'em.

Is that bubblegum? Geez, just the smell puts me on the
    street.

These are divorce papers. I'm sick of wondering what
    she's doing out there. When I get out, I want me a
    clean woman.

I've got an appeal working.

I've got a grievance on file.

I've been talking to a lawyer. We've got a class action
    suit aimed straight at this place.

Sammy's disappeared. Ray's been transferred. Ace got
    shipped off to Mule Creek.

Will you be back on Friday?

Acknowledgements

Several of the poems in this book first appeared in *Adjacent Planes* and *Graceful Exits*, both limited-edition books from Upon Short Notice Press. Special thanks to Miriam Berkley for the use of her beautiful photography. Thanks to the California State Summer School for the Arts for providing long, languid yet riotous summers so that some of these poems could be born. Appreciation to the William James Association; their support for the arts allowed me room to work and still keep the lights on at home. Much appreciation and a deep bow to the American River College English Department and creative writing faculty. Your courage, unshakeable visions and quest for excellence are above and beyond. Thanks to Michael Spurgeon who dared me, and Christian Kiefer who saw to it that I got it done.